Michelle Wie

by Barbara Miller

 HOUGHTON MIFFLIN — BOSTON

PHOTOGRAPHY CREDITS: Cover © David Moir/Reuters/Corbis; 1 © Getty Images: 2 © Gary C. Caskey/epa/Corbis; 3 © Chris Trotman/NewSport/Corbis; 4 © Tetra Images/Alamy; 5 © Stuart Franklin/Getty Images; 6 © Jonathan Ferrey/Getty Images; 7 © David Cannon/Getty Images; 8 © Michael Darden/Associated Press; 9 © Warren LIttle/Getty Images; 10 © DAVID MOIR/Reuters/Corbis

Printed in China

ISBN-13: 978-0-547-02795-1
ISBN-10: 0-547-02795-8

5 6 7 8 9 0940 15 14 13 12 11 10

This is Michelle.

Michelle likes sports.

She likes a sport called golf.

She is good at golf.

This is Michelle's father.

He likes golf, too.

He showed Michelle

how to play golf.

club

ball

tee

Michelle's father
gave her a tee.
He gave her a ball.
He gave her a club.

Michelle's father told her what to do.

Put the tee in the ground.

Put the ball on the tee.

Hit the ball with the club.

Michelle was strong.
She hit the ball far!

Michelle played
and played.
She got better and
better!

Michelle played golf
with kids.
She won those games.

Michelle played golf
with adults.
She won those games!

Michelle is big now.
She still plays golf.
She keeps getting
better and better!

Responding

✓ **TARGET SKILL** **Understanding Characters** What does Michelle Wie do in the story? How does she feel? What does this tell you about Michelle? Make a chart.

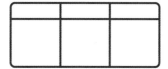

Write About It

Text to World Do you think Michelle Wie is a good friend? Write two sentences to tell what you think and why.

✔ **TARGET SKILL** **Understanding Characters** Tell more about characters.

✔ **TARGET STRATEGY** **Summarize** Stop to tell important ideas as you read.

GENRE **Narrative nonfiction** tells a true story about a topic.